LIFE

THERE'S MORE TO LIFE THEN YOU SEE

YASHARTH KESARWANI

Copyright © Yasharth Kesarwani
All Rights Reserved.

This book has been published with all efforts taken to make the material error-free after the consent of the author. However, the author and the publisher do not assume and hereby disclaim any liability to any party for any loss, damage, or disruption caused by errors or omissions, whether such errors or omissions result from negligence, accident, or any other cause.

While every effort has been made to avoid any mistake or omission, this publication is being sold on the condition and understanding that neither the author nor the publishers or printers would be liable in any manner to any person by reason of any mistake or omission in this publication or for any action taken or omitted to be taken or advice rendered or accepted on the basis of this work. For any defect in printing or binding the publishers will be liable only to replace the defective copy by another copy of this work then available.

You know how it is. You pick up a book, flip to dedication and
find that, once again, the author has
dedicated a book to someone else and not you.
Not this time.
Because we haven't yet met/have only a glancing acquaintance/are
just crazy about each other/haven't seen each other in much too
long/are in some way related/will never meet, but will, I trust,
despite that,
always think fondly of each other..
This one's for you.

With you know what, and you probably know why.
If you were once a student of mine and I asked you to sit down
and quite down in order to get print down,
this one's for you I'm sorry and thankyou. You have made me a
better observer.

This book is dedicated to every overthinker who loves to observe
but hates all the crap that comes with it.

And as always, Mom and Dad...

Who can forget The Almighty her.

Thank you !

Contents

Foreword   *vii*

Preface   *ix*

Acknowledgements   *xi*

Prologue   *xiii*

1. Life   1

2. Memory Trunk   3

3. करीबी   5

4. Across The Veil   6

5. Hope   8

6. Apocalypse   10

7. Chernobyl   13

8. सपने   16

9. Near End   17

10. Death   19

Epilogue   21

Foreword

This book proceedes to take you in a roller-coaster ride which once starts soon will end.

The book starts from "Life" and then moves forward with its turmoil finally ending up with "Death"

The writer is an observant teenage who has inculcated in him to always look the world with a perspective not common and upon reading this you will feel that.

Personally, the author upon first meet seemed to be a boring, egoistic person but gradually with time got to know he is introvert and does not know how to speak up in public. And rest for ego, he is overprotective for his work and life-space. But since he is unable to speak up much I mistakenly took it as ego and proud. Rather he is too friendly and down to Earth if you are able to get close enough.

With every turn of this book I found myself using all the authors tools, hints and ideas to double and triple check the beliefs. And every time I found myself contradicting to my earlier thoughts which were rather too unsual and unchecked. I love the idea that he has written a book that everyone can understand and use to enhance their view towards world.

Preface

"When you are in a hole....."

Most projects start well, and with perfectly good intentions. Before too long, however, many stray from this path, and the project team finds itself overwhelmed with too much to do, too little progress, and criticism from all directions. A standard response to this is to increase the pressure: "Work harder! Work faster! What are you stupid?" This strategy rarely succeeds and often makes a bad situation. even worse. When a project is in trouble, increasing the chaos does not help. To restore order, you must first

Acknowledge that problems exist, and then step back to determine how best to bring the project under control. Todd Williams offers a wealth of proven practices to address this issue in Rescue the Problem Project, which outlines a process for recovering failing projects in clear and unambiguous terms. The steps for recovery-recognition, audit, analysis, negotiation, and re-execution are applicable to troubled projects of nearly any type. The book provides ample guidance to assist you in tailoring the process to your specific needs.

Recovering failing projects requires help. Todd extensively addresses the support you will need, and he offers useful advice on how to secure it. You need help from the team that is presently engaged because its members know what is happening (and more often than not, what to do to fix it). You need help from management, customers, and other project stakeholders. You will probably also need help from outside the project to bring in the fresh perspective that recovery nearly always requires. You need all of this help because restoring a failing project to health inevitably depends on change. If you lack sufficient support resistance to change will ultimately thwart all your recovery efforts. A project in motion tends to remain in motion, even when it is moving in the wrong direction.

Acknowledgements

It takes a large ground crew to help even a small book.

My amazing crew involves all the beings and nature around me believing me for this.

I also want to thank every single person who ever says, "You have to read this book!" to a friend. I don't care if it's this book; I just want people to remind each other how wonderful books are. Particularly, thanks to the people who work at bookstores who do that every day- professionals who can help you find books you will love and are, get this, even better at that than computer programs.

Prologue

Congratulations. The fact that you're reading this means you've taken one giant step closer to surviving from your usual depressing life. Yes, you, standing there leafing through these pages. Do not put this book

down.

I'm dead serious your life could depend on it.

This is my story, the story of my life, but it could just as easily be your story too. We're all in this together;

Trust me on that.

I've never done anything like this, so I'm just going to jump in, and you try to keep up.

Okay, I am Yasharth, I'm seventeen and I'm on a journey to back off the previous loads of thought process with the new one that arrives on path.

A totally experimental and my first publish.

1. Life

Sun has went to touch its shadow,
And twilight is moving to west to eat sunbeam slowly.
Dusk carries an orange legacy which is turning blue leisurely.
And its time to embrace the light ,
Embrace the bright.

So when I lit a candle and watched it proficiently,,
I could feel the warmth which reminds me "LIFE".
And then I saw the wrinkles on candle which I think represent its age ,
It must have paved a long journey to protect the bright to turn to smoke.

Gone through winds several times to prove the cause it is made for,
Gave vision to several blindfolded by nature.
Thats why it rests upon a golden seat with a crown around it.
I then noticed the dancing flame.
Whose reason I knew not ,
And for sure the candle also,
But like a grey head giving a advice

I think it may be telling to learn to be Happy without one.

Then the thought that struck me is just lie life,
The candle loses its spark several times,
But does not forgets to flush again with dazzling light which it brings along,
Finally like life only it ends uo giving its contribution to the WORLD SILENTLY.

2. Memory trunk

My childhood was a dream for sure.
Taunts never stooped upon my mess,
Neither was I moved by tight slaps.
The days were all about being careless about,
Nothing more to worry about.

On a rainy day when slipped on corridor,
Had my first experience to see a swelling head though.
And when my food was spared by names,
That too was some memorable days.

Walking on the balcony wall,
Slipped inside by sake of almighty above,
Was too my part of mischief that time.
Never told anyone till date have I.

Running away from bath in cold,
Causing to fall on a tin sheet below.
With two centimetres in my foot,
Have mark of stitches still fooling there in row.

Amid these all thoughts that been,
I am not able to write the short ones,

With glee unknown that covered my face.

Meaningless was the life which could nothing more be meaningful,

I willfully wish that for now but forcefully cannot have that now.

My childhood was not all this so small,

But I have a big truck kept hidden from you all.

3. करीबी

चुप हुआ क्यों अगर ये तुम जाते नहीं,
किस हक से हमें करीबी बतलाते हो ।

चेहरे पे शकिन अगर नहीं पहचान पाते हो,
किस हक से हमें करीबी बतलाते हो ।

काम निकलवाते समय ही याद हम आ रहे,
फिर किस हक से हमें करीबी बतला रहे ।

फायदा हो उठा रहे उस भरी सभा में,
पता नहीं किस हक से हमें करीबी बतला रहे ।

सच में बता उनमें तुम ना आ रहे,
फिर न जाने किस हक से हमें करीबी बतला रहे ।

फासला है अभी बहुत अभी करें आने में,
सोचने को अब बाकी है क्या इन प्रश्नों के आ जाने से ।

4. Across the veil

Leaning shadows on the lane,
Wavering thoughts have ceased along.
Now that I know nothing's up,
Scribbles roaming right inside my head.
Powering me to ponder upon,
The diguise must have been all along.
All along the space that fed your mind,
To see me all throughout the limpid veil.
Wasn't it a well planned game,
You should give that thought a name.
Witnessing the stone drear,
Upon the face which looked me up,
Facing the truth beneath the veil,
To find out there's more to be passionate about.
Tryn to be a stock out there,
But that anxiety of me pulls all along,
To break the bar has been its stride,
Never lets me lead a usual life.
Retarded to thougts to move aside,
To go public was not my type,
Still have my own colour,
still have my own belief,
My wings are not cut upon.

Running through the lane ofcourse,

Whom do you think are those leaning shadows then all across?

•7•

5. Hope

In search of unknown,
Lost cities of hope.
My path heeds to move along,
To move along the woven slope.
Targeted by armed shadow,
To change the lit view of scope,
To change the mind in view of thought,
Was never negligible to be cared at all.

Tending to move with crossing lane,
Was never my fiend cluttered in thoughts.
Neither let it overcome,
To clog my wailing sixth alarm.
Pioneering to the thoughts indeed,
Was nowhere to be seen.
Pious acts of silence in hope,
Mourn upon the end of none,
Giving the soul its bright with peace.
But there was shut past never,
This truth should be instilled upon,
Never to try playing with hope ever.

Hope can be a fatal sport,

Neither did i lose one nor could find one.

Losers of hope,

Losers of war,

Waiting for the timely alarm,

To wake up and find again,

The one lost in hope to rejoice again.

Screams will still knock your earshell,

Following the path will help you none.

Imprisonment is not over yet,

The nightmare of hope will be with you all along.

6. Apocalypse

We dont know what's the future,
We dont know whats coming up,
I still don't convince that futures safe as we are heading it
to,
Dreams laiden by sand and starving to death to hold up
for answer still unlistened , haunt me !

Learning to breathe through the cloth against the sand
that fills me up.
Mirages, mirages do i see again,
Fed up to see those seducive waters away,
The lighting of thunder mere meters far haunt me to shiver
from tip to toe,
The waters ending up with hopes ceasing.
Am still confused and puzzled...
Intoxicated by mere bizzareness,
Shall guide me to soberness , I guess.

Graves am i not able to see ,
But corpses have been throughout my vision.
So dark that fail to feel ,
Fail to feel alive again.

Gliding alone ,
Gliding through space ,
It may be a haunting nightmare , I guess.
Piling up all what have i seen ,
To bind up for deaths have I seen.

No time to regret upon,
To live in the realm that paved me up.
Doomed to death,
Doomed to fight ,
Cannot be more eager for life.

Hope for cure ,
Hope for truth ,
Lived in shattering lies for ages unknown.
Falling for life stuck in death ,
its a trap maybe I guess.
Scorched by Sun to death,
Move me up close to the clouds some left.

Shrunken life and blinding light ,
Is all i see through the day,
Falling for dark is a myth,
As you can see storms waiting away.

Hope not to hope ever,
It gives you chance to take cover,

Upon the end which could be smooth ,
Was pelted all by hope.

Silence be upon my lips ,
Upon meeting the endless end.
Struggle not to strangle me up ,
Upon meeting the god of death.

Tested for life,
Tested to survive,
I dont know how many miles to go alive.
Able to see world against me,
Able to see whats growing up.
Hope to meet an old friend ,
Which i hope does not eat me up,
The halt of ellixir of life is seen.
Running running and only running ,
For life to see,
For days of joys we dreamt of ,
For days of life we dreamt of.

7. Chernobyl

The end is near.
The end is sure,
Would not want it to be man made for sure.

Radioactive is the air,
What could be more worse than that.
Melting through and soaring breaths,
Penetrating me to shed my skin.
My scream heard nowhere at all,
All Silenced by wailing alarm.
Vomitting blood and burning as hell,
Breating along the radioactive ash.

The air is glowing.
Cherenkov effect they said,
But it was a warning to be more precise.
They did not evacuated the town in time,
Causing to murder a million alives.

5.6 was the roentgen per second ,
Piling up to be more than thousands per hour.
The medics could not be more helpless ,
Seeing an entire town turn down to ash and dust.

Saw handling a part of metal with hand ,
Leading to death within an hour.
No need to regret upon ,
We too will be soon dumped in the toxic trash.
For sure no time to pick and fix up the mess,
The matter was of pride , else
Could have saved many lives along.

The reactor was on fire if right ,
The firemen were struggling to put it out,
Slowly they all fell to ground ,
Ended up bloodshed in the battleground.
Dont know worth was their sacrifice ,
Could have lived happily with their wives .
The scientist still believed in books ,
It can never explode through bricks,
But the truth was he keeping aside,
Responsible for death of multiple lives.
Wailing of sirens and alarms ,
Were picercing ears along slow decay of radioair.

Many are sleeping ,
Many on road (The bridge of death),
To see the great fire show ,
Praying for them to be safe but who knew ,
They were also unwilling involved in part of the mess.
The toxic dust is part of air,

No one can check that up .
Thanatos is waiting by ,
To take its passengers without fear.

The catastrophe outspread itself miles away.
Learning to survive with it was one option to be seen ,
Else bury yourself in the ground else the turmoil of
dreadful death peeked on from now,
Radiation contamination was the term ,
Better to dozing off with drear.
The scene was bleak and bitter,
Sudden slow unreal death overpowered with fear.

Maxed out on dozimeter,
Still veiling for pride was their game.
Sabotage was their guess,
But the question of mishandling was neither took off yet,
Though more close was carelessness and the pride that
stuck.
Whatsoever may be cause ,
We cannot bring back the gone.
The blame game is not started yet ,
The official will checkmate eveyone ,
Giving the deaths an integer ,
Questioning their death , was it worth?

8. सपने

सपने अब भी वही हैं।
उम्मीदों से हूं बस थक रहा,
शब्दों से हूं बस झुक रहा हूँ।
ठहरने का अन्देशा दे रहे मुझ,
या खींच के पटकने में यूं हो सब तुले।
तारकि से हैं सब बदल गए,
विश्वास खुद यूं कुचल गये।
बेचैन हूं मैं कुछ जरा,
खामोशी से यूं बंधा।
शोक किस बात का जो था नही कभी मेरा,
जी रहा हूं मैं अभी, कल का हो क्या पता।

9. Near end

These days have been too dark.

Too dark have been my thoughts,

The thoughts that have been on head,

Have power to summon upon,

The evil God Satan ever,

Fallen upon to crook and evil,

Trying to vanish the world forever.

Not worth was the cause,

Also need some servents to pray me afterall.

Surreal is the world I see,

The graves also have destiny,

Far more the land bears,

The sea also does not spare.

Fright with dark is growing too great,

Dreaming of skulls to wave me in day.

Skeletons to go like vikings in row,

Killing along the mass in woah,

Spectating the sport they play,

Would really appreciate the worthy though.

Doing Vodoo is much of fun,

If you know whom upon to instill along.

Pandemic was none the less to finish an entire race above,

But the monkeys have evolved to far,

To cheat on to nature,
And get framed beside dinosaurs.
Disturbed by all these thoughts that come,
Would have been better if simply WW3 begin.

10. Death

Leaning on the rocking chair,
Last time is now near.
An endless sleep awaits for me.
An endless run has ceased along.
Clock has thus the same time now,
Awaiting for peace to come by now.
Eager to see the creator soon,
Eyes cannot be more tired,
Cannot be more dead now.
Lived a life full,
Scenes of this world still unstill,
Beneath the eyelids upon closing,
Like this all happened only yesterday.
All beings that were a part,
To complete this novel of my life apart,
I thank you all for being a part,
Life would have been sorrowful else.
Bidding you all a happy adieu,
Let me now rest in peace for now.

Epilogue

"I believe you."

The story is over,

yet it doesn't mean.

I have stopped reading it.

It doesn't mean

I have stopped writing about it.

It doesn't mean

it is over for me;

for you once told me love would never end.

"I believed you,"

wrote the epilogue.

-Timothy Joshua